The Legacy of the Knight Templars in Portugal: Guardians of Faith and Warriors of History

Marc Ferrari

COPYRIGHT

QUOTE

"Praise be to the Lord my rock.

Who train my hand for war

My fingers for battle"

Psalm 144:1

Table of Contents

THE ORIGINS OF THE KNIGHT TEMPLARS AND THEIR ARRIVAL IN PORTUGAL

Hello there, let's dive deeper into the fascinating history of the Knight Templars and their arrival in Portugal!

The Knight Templars, also known as the Poor Fellow-Soldiers of Christ and of the Temple of Solomon, were founded in 1119 by a group of nine French knights in Jerusalem. Their primary mission was to protect Christian pilgrims traveling to the Holy Land. The order quickly gained prominence and became one of the most powerful institutions in Europe, with branches in many countries and a vast network of properties and churches.

The Templars had their own hierarchy and rules, and their members took vows of poverty, chastity, and obedience. They wore distinctive white mantles with a red cross and were known for their bravery and military prowess.

In 1128, the Templars were officially recognized by the Catholic Church and became exempt from local jurisdiction, which meant they were only accountable to the Pope. This status allowed the order to expand rapidly and to amass great wealth and influence.

Now, let's fast forward to the 12th century, when the Templars arrived in Portugal. At the time, the country was still in the process of consolidating its power, and King Afonso Henriques was at the forefront of this effort. The Templars were invited to help defend the newly formed kingdom and to assist in the Reconquista, the campaign to drive the Moors out of the Iberian Peninsula.

The Templars quickly established themselves in Portugal and were granted lands and privileges by the king. The first Templar commandery in Portugal was founded in 1142 in the town of Soure, in the central region of the country. Other commanderies soon followed, and the order became an important part of the Portuguese military and religious landscape.

The Templars played a key role in many battles and campaigns in Portugal, including the Siege of Lisbon in 1147 and the Battle of Ourique. They also participated in the establishment of several monasteries and churches, including the Monastery of Santa Maria da Vitória in Batalha and the Convent of Christ in Tomar, which are still considered some of the greatest examples of Portuguese architecture and art.

The arrival of the Templars in Portugal marked a turning point in the country's history. The order brought with it a new model of military and religious organization, which had a profound impact on Portuguese society and culture. The Templars' legacy in Portugal can still be seen today in the many monuments, traditions, and stories that have been passed down through the centuries.

Overall, the Knight Templars' arrival in Portugal was a pivotal moment in the country's history. The order's influence on Portuguese culture and society is still felt to this day, and their legacy will continue to be a source of fascination and inspiration for generations to come.

THE PORTUGUESE TEMPLARS' ROLE IN THE RECONQUISTA

Welcome to this chapter on the Portuguese Templars' role in the Reconquista. In the previous chapter, we briefly touched on the fact that the Templars were instrumental in the defense of the newly formed Portuguese kingdom, but in this chapter, we'll dive deeper into the specific ways in which they contributed to the Reconquista.

Firstly, it's important to understand the context in which the Reconquista was taking place. The Moors, who were Muslims from North Africa and the Middle East, had conquered much of the Iberian Peninsula in the 8th century, and they had held onto it for centuries. The Christian kingdoms of the north, including Portugal, were determined to push the Moors out and reclaim their land.

The Templars, who had been established as a military order in Jerusalem in 1119, quickly gained a reputation as some of the finest warriors in Europe. Their order was officially recognized by the Church in 1139, and just a few years later, in 1143, they were invited by King Afonso Henriques to assist in the defense of Portugal.

The Templars' arrival in Portugal marked a turning point in the Reconquista. The order's members were highly skilled and experienced warriors, and they had a deep commitment to the cause of defending Christendom. They also had a unique system of organization and training, which allowed them to operate effectively in a variety of environments.

One of the most notable battles in which the Templars played a crucial role was the Siege of Lisbon in 1147. The city had been under Muslim control for centuries, but with the assistance of the Templars, the Christians were able to take the city and establish a foothold in the south.

But the Templars' contribution to the Reconquista wasn't limited to the battlefield. They also played an important role in the colonization of newly conquered territories, often establishing new settlements and fortresses to help consolidate Christian control. The Templars' commanderies, which were scattered throughout Portugal, served as bases of operations for their military and religious activities.

The Templars' involvement in the Reconquista wasn't solely focused on military and political matters, either. They also contributed to the spread of Christianity in Portugal, building and maintaining many churches and monasteries throughout the country. The order's members were known for their piety and devotion to the Church, and they played a significant role in the religious life of the Portuguese people.

One of the most significant contributions of the Templars to the Reconquista was the development of a new style of military organization. The order's members were organized into small, highly trained units that could operate independently and effectively in a variety of environments. This model of military organization was a departure from the feudal armies that were common in Europe at the time, and it proved to be highly effective in the context of the Reconquista.

Despite their successes, the Portuguese Templars were not without their challenges. Their vast wealth and power made them a target of envy and suspicion, and rumors of heresy and corruption began to circulate. These rumors ultimately led to the order's downfall, as we'll explore in later chapters.

Nevertheless, the Portuguese Templars made a significant contribution to the Reconquista. Their skill in battle, their commitment to the cause of defending Christendom, and their development of a new style of military organization helped pave the way for the eventual reconquest of the Iberian Peninsula. The Templars' legacy in Portugal is still felt today, and their contribution to the country's history is remembered with pride.

THE FOUNDING OF THE ORDER OF CHRIST AND THE PORTUGUESE TEMPLARS' REBRANDING

As we discussed earlier, the founding of the Order of Christ was a response to the suppression of the Templars throughout Europe. While other European countries were quick to take action against the order, Portugal refused to follow suit. King Dinis, who was a close ally of the Templars, saw an opportunity to bring the order under his direct control, and to benefit from its wealth and power.

The Order of Christ was established in 1319, and it was granted many of the assets and privileges that had been held by the Templars. The order was given vast estates, and it was exempt from many of the taxes and obligations that other organizations were subject to.

The Order of Christ was more than just a continuation of the Templars, however. It was also a rebranding, designed to distance the order from the rumors and suspicions that had plagued the Templars. The order adopted a new symbol, the cross of Christ, which was seen as a more appropriate symbol for a religious order. The order also made some changes to the way it operated, shifting its focus from military matters to religious matters.

One of the key changes that the Order of Christ made was to its organizational structure. While the Templars had been organized into a single order with a centralized leadership, the Order of Christ was organized into a series of commanderies, each with its own local leader. This allowed the order to be more flexible and adaptable, and it made it easier to respond to the changing needs of the country.

Despite these changes, the Order of Christ remained true to the spirit of the Templars. The order's members were still committed to the defence of the faith, and they continued to play an important role in the Reconquista. The order's members were also known for their piety and their devotion to the Church, and they built many churches and monasteries throughout Portugal.

Over time, the Order of Christ became one of the most important and influential organizations in Portugal. The order played a role in the country's exploration and colonization of new territories, and it helped to shape the culture and society of the country.

The Order of Christ also had a significant impact on the arts and culture of Portugal. The order supported many artists and craftsmen, and it commissioned numerous works of art and architecture. Some of the most famous examples of this are the Manueline style of architecture, which was heavily influenced by the Order of Christ.

The founding of the Order of Christ was a pivotal moment in the history of the Templars in Portugal. The order allowed the Templars to continue their work, while also distancing them from the rumors and suspicions that had led to their downfall in other parts of Europe. The Order of Christ went on to become one of the most important and influential organizations in Portugal, and its legacy is still felt in the country today.

THE TEMPLARS' MILITARY AND POLITICAL INFLUENCE IN PORTUGAL

The Templars' reputation as skilled warriors and fearless fighters was well earned, and their military prowess was a key factor in many of Portugal's most famous battles. During the Reconquista, for example, the Templars fought alongside other Christian armies to push the Muslims out of Portugal and establish a Christian presence in the region. They were instrumental in many key battles, including the Battle of Ourique in 1139, which is considered a pivotal moment in the country's history.

In addition to their battlefield success, the Templars also played an important role in the construction and maintenance of fortresses and castles throughout Portugal. These strongholds were essential for defending the country against invading forces, and the Templars' skill in engineering and architecture made them ideal candidates for overseeing their construction. Some of the most famous of these fortresses include the Castle of Almourol, which was built on a small island in the Tagus River, and the Castle of Tomar, which served as the order's headquarters in Portugal.

The Templars' influence in Portuguese politics was also significant. The order was closely aligned with the royal family, and its members held many important positions in the government. King Dinis, for example, was a strong supporter of the Templars and worked closely with them to implement important reforms in the country. The Templars were also involved in the founding of Portugal's first university, the University of Coimbra, and played a key role in many other important initiatives and reforms throughout the country's history.

Despite their many accomplishments, however, the Templars were not without their detractors. Some critics accused the order of being too powerful and too influential, and there were concerns about their wealth and their role in Portuguese affairs. These criticisms eventually led to the suppression of the order throughout Europe, and the founding of the Order of Christ in Portugal. This new order was established in 1319 and was tasked with taking over many of the Templars' functions and properties in the country.

Even with the founding of the Order of Christ, however, the Templars' legacy in Portugal continued to be felt for centuries. Many of the fortresses and castles they built still stand today, and their influence on Portuguese society and culture is still evident in many ways. From the traditions and customs they established to the institutions they helped to create, the Templars played an important role in shaping Portugal's history, and their impact is still felt in the country today.

THE PORTUGUESE TEMPLARS' RELATIONSHIP WITH THE CROWN AND THE CHURCH

The relationship between the Portuguese Templars, the crown, and the church was a complex one that evolved over time. At the beginning of their history in Portugal, the Templars were granted many privileges by the monarchy, and their loyalty to the king was unwavering. This close relationship allowed the order to grow in power and influence, becoming a key player in the political landscape of Portugal during the Middle Ages.

The Templars' military prowess and political influence were significant, and their role in the Reconquista was crucial in reclaiming Portugal from Islamic rule. Their fortresses and castles, strategically placed along the border with Spain, helped to defend Portugal from the constant threat of invasion. Their reputation as fierce warriors and their religious zeal inspired many to join their cause, and they became a symbol of national pride and identity.

As the order grew in power and influence, tensions began to arise between the Templars and the monarchy. Some members of the nobility felt threatened by the order's wealth and influence, and accused them of using their power to further their own interests. These tensions eventually led to a rift between the Templars and the crown, culminating in the arrest and suppression of the order by King Denis in the early 14th century.

At the same time, the church was also beginning to take a more critical view of the Templars. Reports of questionable practices and accusations of heresy had led to an investigation into the order's activities, and eventually to their suppression by Pope Clement V. This was a devastating blow to the Templars, and many members were arrested, tortured, and killed.

Despite the suppression of the Templars, their legacy in Portugal continued to be felt. The Order of Christ was established in Portugal in 1319, and many former Templars joined its ranks. The new order was closely aligned with both the monarchy and the church, and played an important role in Portuguese politics and culture in the centuries to come. The Templars' fortresses and castles still stand today as important cultural and historical landmarks, and their influence on Portuguese culture and society is still evident in many ways.

The Templars' relationship with the crown and the church was a complicated one, characterized by both loyalty and tension. Their role in the Reconquista and their military and political influence in Portugal was significant, and their legacy can still be felt in the country today. While the suppression of the order was a devastating blow, it did not erase the impact that the Templars had on Portugal's history and culture.

THE TEMPLARS' FINANCIAL POWER AND BANKING SYSTEM

The Templars' financial power and banking system were truly groundbreaking for their time, and their influence can still be felt today. Their system was built on a foundation of trust and reliability, which allowed them to establish themselves as a leading financial institution throughout Europe and the Middle East.

At the heart of the Templars' financial system was the concept of credit, which allowed them to lend money to individuals and institutions throughout Europe. They were known for their honesty and integrity, and their reputation for financial stability led many wealthy individuals and organizations to entrust them with their money. This allowed the Templars to accumulate vast amounts of wealth over time, which they used to finance their military and political endeavors.

One of the most significant innovations of the Templars' banking system was the use of letters of credit. These were essentially promissory notes that could be used to transfer money across long distances. This was a revolutionary concept at the time, as it allowed for the safe and efficient transfer of funds without the need for physical transportation. The Templars' letters of credit were widely accepted throughout Europe and the Middle East, which made them a valuable tool for commerce and trade.

In addition to their banking activities, the Templars also acquired vast amounts of property and land throughout

Europe. They were given many privileges by the Pope and European monarchs, which allowed them to acquire land and establish new sources of income. They also engaged in trade and commerce, which allowed them to accumulate even more wealth over time.

The Templars' financial power was not without controversy, however. Their wealth and influence made them a target for accusations of corruption and greed, and many members of the nobility began to feel threatened by their power. In addition, their association with heretical movements and secret societies led to rumors and conspiracy theories that still persist to this day.

Despite these challenges, the Templars' innovations in banking and credit paved the way for modern banking systems, and their vast wealth and influence helped to shape the course of European history. Today, the Templars' legacy in finance and banking is still felt, and their influence can be seen in the many financial institutions and practices that we use today. Without their groundbreaking contributions to the world of finance, the global economy as we know it today may not have been possible.

THE TEMPLARS' ROLE IN PORTUGUESE ART AND ARCHITECTURE

The Templars' impact on Portuguese art and architecture was significant and long-lasting. Their legacy is still evident in many of the country's most impressive works of art and architecture, which continue to inspire and fascinate visitors to this day.

Perhaps the most notable example of the Templars' influence on Portuguese art and architecture is the Convento de Cristo, located in the town of Tomar. This stunning complex was built by the Templars in the 12th century, and it became the headquarters of the Order of Christ after the dissolution of the Templars. The convent boasts a fascinating blend of Gothic, Manueline, and Renaissance architectural styles, which reflect the evolving tastes and sensibilities of the Templars and their successors.

The Convento de Cristo is also home to many exquisite examples of Templar art, including frescoes, paintings, and sculptures. One of the most notable features of the convent is the magnificent window in the chapterhouse, which is considered a masterpiece of Manueline art. This intricate window is adorned with carvings of animals, leaves, and other natural forms, which demonstrate the Templars' love of nature and their belief in the beauty and majesty of God's creations.

The Castle of Almourol is another impressive example of Templar architecture in Portugal. This stunning fortress was built on a small island in the Tagus River in the 12th century, and it remains one of the most impressive and well-preserved castles in the country. The castle's sturdy walls and imposing towers are a testament to the Templars' military prowess, while its ornate carvings and other decorative features demonstrate their artistic sensibilities.

The Templars were also patrons of the arts, commissioning many beautiful paintings, sculptures, and other works of art to adorn their churches and other religious buildings. Many of these works of art have been preserved and are on display in museums and galleries throughout Portugal. For example, the Museu Nacional de Arte Antiga in Lisbon houses a significant collection of medieval and Renaissance art, including works commissioned by the Templars.

In addition to their contributions to art and architecture, the Templars were also known for their skill in masonry and stonecutting. Their mastery of these techniques allowed them to create some of the most beautiful and intricate architectural details of their time. Many of these details can be seen in the elaborate carvings and stonework of the Convento de Cristo and other Templar buildings.

Knights Templar Sites in Portugal

The Knights Templar left an indelible mark on Portugal's landscape, as they constructed numerous castles, churches, and fortresses throughout the country. These structures have stood the test of time and are now a testament to the Templars' architectural and engineering skills, as well as their military might.

Here are some of the most notable Knights Templar sites in Portugal:

-Tomar Castle: This castle was the headquarters of the Knights Templar in Portugal and is one of the best-preserved medieval castles in the country. It is also home to the famous Convent of Christ, which was built by the Templars and is a UNESCO World Heritage Site.

-Almourol Castle: This small but impressive castle is situated on a small island in the middle of the Tagus River. It was built by the Templars in the 12th century and is now a popular tourist attraction.

-Castelo de Pombal: This castle was built by the Templars in the 12th century to defend the city against the Moors. It is now a popular tourist attraction and has been restored to its former glory.

-Castelo de Monsanto: This castle was built by the Templars in the 12th century and is one of the most impressive in the country. It is situated on a hilltop and offers spectacular views of the surrounding countryside.

-Castelo de Soure: This castle was built by the Templars in the 12th century and is a good example of their military architecture. It is situated in the center of the town of Soure and is now a national monument.

-Convento de Cristo, Tomar: This is one of the most important Templar sites in Portugal, and it is now a UNESCO World Heritage Site. The Convent of Christ was originally built as a fortress by the Templars and was later converted into a monastery.

-Castle of Idanha-a-Nova: This castle was built by the Templars in the 13th century and was an important defensive stronghold against the Moors. It is now a popular tourist attraction.

-Castle of Ourém: This castle was built by the Templars in the 12th century and is now a national monument. It is situated on a hill overlooking the town of Ourém and is a popular tourist attraction.

-Castle of Penela: This castle was built by the Templars in the 12th century and is now a national monument. It is situated on a hill overlooking the town of Penela and is a popular tourist attraction.

-Castle of Zêzere: This castle was built by the Templars in the 13th century and is now a national monument. It is situated on a hill overlooking the Zêzere River and is a popular tourist attraction.

The Knights Templar played a significant role in shaping Portugal's history, and their legacy lives on through the castles, churches, and fortresses they built. These sites are not only a testament to their military prowess and engineering skills but also provide an insight into the medieval world in which they lived. Visitors to Portugal can still experience the Templars' legacy by exploring these impressive sites, which offer a glimpse into a bygone era.

THE TEMPLARS' PARTICIPATION IN THE CRUSADES

The role of the Templars in the Crusades was a crucial part of their history, and it helped to define their reputation as some of the greatest warriors of the Middle Ages. These campaigns were driven by the desire to reclaim the Holy Land from Muslim control, and the Templars were at the forefront of the struggle.

The first Knight templars campaign in the holy land

The First Crusade was launched in 1096, and by 1099, the Christian forces had successfully taken Jerusalem. The Holy City, however, was in a precarious position, surrounded by hostile Muslim territories. The new Christian Kingdom of Jerusalem required a constant influx of military support from Europe to maintain its hold on the region. In response to this need, various orders of knights were founded, including the Order of the Temple, or the Knights Templar.

The Knights Templar were founded in 1119 by a group of French knights, who took monastic vows and pledged to defend pilgrims traveling to and from the Holy Land. They soon became one of the most powerful and influential military orders of the Crusader era, and their reputation for valor and piety spread throughout Europe.

In 1129, the Knights Templar received official recognition from the Catholic Church, which granted them a rule of conduct and various privileges, including the right to build their own churches and to be exempt from all taxes and tithes. The order rapidly grew in wealth and influence, with members from all over Europe joining its ranks.

The first significant military campaign of the Knights Templar in the Holy Land took place in 1137, when they joined the forces of King Fulk of Jerusalem and Count Raymond of Tripoli in an attack on the Muslim-held fortress of Barin. The knights distinguished themselves in the battle, and their prowess in combat won them great respect and admiration from their fellow Crusaders.

Over the next few decades, the Knights Templar played a key role in the defense of the Kingdom of Jerusalem, fighting in numerous battles and skirmishes against Muslim forces. They also engaged in various construction projects, building fortifications, churches, and other buildings to strengthen the Christian presence in the region.

The most famous engagement of the Knights Templar in the Holy Land took place in 1187, when Muslim forces led by Saladin captured Jerusalem. The fall of the Holy City was a major blow to the Crusaders, and many knights, including the Templars, vowed to retake the city at all costs.

In 1191, a large Christian army led by King Richard the Lionheart of England and King Philip II of France arrived in the Holy Land to launch a new offensive. The Knights Templar played a significant role in this campaign, fighting in several key battles, including the famous Battle of Arsuf in which they played a critical role in securing a Christian victory.

Despite their bravery and dedication, the Knights Templar were unable to prevent the gradual loss of Christian territory in the Holy Land. By the late 13th century, the Christian presence in the region had been reduced to a few scattered outposts and fortresses, and the order's focus shifted to defending these remaining strongholds.

In 1291, the last Christian stronghold in the Holy Land, the city of Acre, fell to Muslim forces. With their mission to defend the Holy Land seemingly at an end, the Knights Templar shifted their focus to other endeavors, including banking, trade, and diplomacy.

The first Knight Templars campaign in the Holy Land was marked by valor, dedication, and a deep commitment to the defense of Christianity. The knights' military prowess and piety won them widespread admiration, and their legacy continues to be felt to this day.

The first Portuguese Knight Templars

The first Portuguese Knight Templars were a group of knights who joined the Order of the Temple, a military order of the Catholic Church founded in Jerusalem in the 12th century. The exact date of their establishment in Portugal is unclear, but it is believed to have been in the early 12th century.

The Portuguese Templars were initially established as a small group of knights who had fought in the Crusades and were inspired by the ideals of the Order of the Temple.

These knights were granted land and other privileges by the Portuguese monarch, and they quickly gained a reputation for their military prowess and their commitment to the defense of the Christian faith.

One of the most prominent of these early Portuguese Templars was Gualdim Pais, who was appointed the Grand Master of the Order in Portugal in 1147. Gualdim Pais led the Templars in a number of battles against the Moors in Portugal and was instrumental in the establishment of the Kingdom of Portugal.

Under Gualdim Pais and subsequent Grand Masters, the Portuguese Templars grew in both size and influence. They continued to be actively involved in the Crusades, and they played a significant role in the Reconquista, the period of Christian reconquest of the Iberian Peninsula from the Moors. The Portuguese Templars also became known for their military and political power, their financial influence, and their cultural and architectural contributions to Portuguese society.

Despite their successes, the Templars were also accused of heresy and other crimes, and the order was ultimately dissolved by Pope Clement V in the early 14th century. However, the legacy of the Portuguese Templars lived on, and their influence can still be seen in modern-day Portugal, as well as in the history and mythology of the Knight Templars around the world.

Knight Templars contribution to the Crusades

The Templars were a perfect fit for the Crusades because of their military prowess and discipline. They were skilled horsemen and expert fighters, and they had honed their abilities through years of training and experience. As a result, they quickly earned a reputation for their bravery and were trusted to lead the charge in many battles.

Their contributions to the Crusades were not just limited to their military power, however. The Templars also played an important role in the logistical aspects of the campaigns. They had a vast network of estates and properties throughout Europe, which allowed them to raise large amounts of money and supplies for the Crusader armies. They also acted as bankers and financiers, providing loans and credit to other knights and soldiers who needed it.

In addition to their military and financial contributions, the Templars also played a crucial role in the cultural and religious aspects of the Crusades. They were known for their devotion to their faith, and their presence on the battlefield was seen as a symbol of the strength and resolve of the Christian forces. They also took it upon themselves to protect and care for Christian pilgrims who were traveling to the Holy Land, providing them with safe passage and medical care when needed.

Despite their many contributions, the Templars were not immune to controversy during the Crusades. Some accused them of being too powerful and wealthy, and of using their influence for their own gain. There were also accusations of heresy and immoral practices, although these were largely unfounded.

The Templars' participation in the Crusades was not without cost. Many of their members lost their lives in battle, and their resources were stretched thin by the ongoing campaigns. Nonetheless, they continued to fight on, driven by their commitment to their faith and their duty to defend it.

Today, the legacy of the Templars in the Crusades can be seen in the many works of art and literature that celebrate their exploits. Their story has captured the imaginations of people all over the world, and they remain one of the most fascinating and mysterious groups of the Middle Ages. Their bravery, dedication, and skill on the battlefield continue to inspire people to this day, and their contributions to the history of the Crusades cannot be overstated.

THE TEMPLARS' ALLEGED HERESIES AND THE CHARGES OF WITCHCRAFT

The accusations of heresy and witchcraft against the Templars are some of the most controversial and fascinating aspects of their history. While the charges were largely unfounded, they played a significant role in the downfall of the order.

The accusations of heresy were particularly troubling, as they implied that the Templars held beliefs that were considered to be contrary to the official doctrine of the Church. Some of the accusations were quite specific, such as claims that the Templars denied the divinity of Christ or worshipped idols. Others were more vague and sensational, such as allegations of sodomy, devil worship, and the desecration of Christian symbols.

The charges of witchcraft were equally troubling, and were a common accusation during the Middle Ages. The idea was that the Templars had used magic or sorcery to gain their wealth and power, and had made a pact with the devil. There were also allegations of obscene rituals and other sacrilegious practices.

While there is no evidence to support these accusations, it is important to understand the context in which they were made. The Templars were a powerful and influential organization, and their secretive nature and immense wealth made them the subject of suspicion and fear. Furthermore, King Philip IV of France had a personal vendetta against the Templars, and may have used the charges of heresy and witchcraft as a pretext to seize their assets.

King Philip IV of France and the Templars

Philip IV, also known as Philip the Fair, became king of France in 1285 at the age of 17. He was a shrewd and ambitious monarch who sought to consolidate his power and increase his wealth. One of his most notorious acts was the suppression of the Knights Templar.

The Templars had long been an influential and wealthy organization, with their vast holdings of land and treasure making them a powerful force in Europe. However, by the early 14th century, the order had fallen out of favor with many monarchs, who saw them as a threat to their power.

Philip IV was one such monarch. He had become deeply indebted to the Templars after borrowing large sums of money from them to finance his wars. However, instead of repaying the debt, he began to view the Templars as a potential rival to his power. In 1307, he began a campaign to discredit and destroy the order.

Philip began by ordering the arrest of all the Templars in France on charges of heresy, blasphemy, and other crimes. The charges were largely fabricated, but Philip used them as a pretext to seize the order's property and wealth. He also pressured Pope Clement V to launch an investigation into the order, hoping to use the papacy's influence to destroy the Templars once and for all.

The investigation culminated in the Council of Vienne in 1312, where the pope officially dissolved the order and confiscated its assets. Many of the Templars were tortured and forced to confess to crimes they did not commit, and some were even burned at the stake as heretics. The few Templars who managed to escape fled to other countries, where they blended into other orders or went into hiding.

The consequences of these accusations were severe. Many Templars were arrested, tortured, and executed, and the order was eventually disbanded by the Church. The Templars' reputation was forever tarnished by the allegations of heresy and witchcraft, and their legacy remains shrouded in mystery and speculation.

Today, historians continue to debate the veracity of the charges against the Templars. Some argue that the accusations were entirely fabricated, while others believe that there may have been some truth to them. Regardless of the truth, the Templars' alleged heresies and witchcraft are a testament to the enduring fascination and mystique of this enigmatic order.

THE ARREST AND DISSOLUTION OF THE ORDER IN PORTUGAL

The arrest and dissolution of the Order of the Templars in Portugal was a dramatic and tumultuous event that changed the course of the country's history. At the time, the Templars were one of the most powerful and influential organizations in Portugal, with immense wealth and political influence. However, as the 14th century wore on, the order's fortunes began to decline, and it fell out of favor with the Pope and the kings of Europe.

In 1307, King Philip IV of France launched a devastating campaign against the Templars, accusing them of heresy, idolatry, and witchcraft. The charges were largely baseless, but they proved effective in undermining the order's reputation and support. Pope Clement V ordered an investigation, and in 1312, the order was officially dissolved by the Church. Many Templars were arrested, tortured, and executed, and their assets were seized by the Church and the kings of Europe.

The Knights Templar were once one of the most powerful and influential organizations in medieval Europe, but their sudden downfall was equally swift and spectacular. While the exact reasons for their fall from grace remain a matter of debate, the role played by Pope Clement V in their eventual dissolution is considered crucial. In this chapter, we will explore the reasons why the Pope went against the Knights Templar.

One of the most widely cited reasons for the Pope's

opposition to the Templars was their increasing power and influence. The Templars had become one of the wealthiest and most influential organizations in Europe, with vast land holdings, vast wealth and a large standing army. Their military prowess and political influence had become so significant that they were virtually beyond the control of the church or any other secular authority. The Templars were essentially a state within a state, and their unchecked power and influence had made them a potential threat to the existing social and political order.

Another factor that may have played a role in the Pope's decision was the issue of debt owed to the Templars. Many monarchs and nobles had borrowed heavily from the Templars to finance their wars and other endeavors. As a result, the Templars had become one of the most powerful financial institutions in Europe, and the debt owed to them was a significant burden on many kingdoms. By moving against the Templars, the Pope may have hoped to relieve some of the financial pressure on these nations.

There were also persistent rumors and allegations of heresy and moral corruption within the order. Some accused the Templars of engaging in blasphemous rituals and practices, while others claimed that they were secretly promoting unorthodox religious ideas. Although there is little evidence to support these accusations, they were enough to cast a shadow over the order and make them a target of suspicion.

The fact that the Templars had become increasingly involved in the politics of the Holy Land may also have played a role in the Pope's decision. The Templars had been founded as a religious order dedicated to the defense of Christian holy sites in the Holy Land, but over time they had become heavily involved in the politics of the region. This had led to tensions with other Christian and Muslim groups, and may have contributed to the Pope's perception of the order as a destabilizing force.

Finally, there may have been personal motives behind the Pope's decision. Some scholars believe that the Pope was simply looking for a way to consolidate his own power and assert his authority over the powerful and wealthy order. By moving against the Templars, he could demonstrate his power and authority, while also bringing the wealth and resources of the order under his control.

While the exact reasons for the Pope's opposition to the Templars remain a matter of debate, there were likely a number of factors that contributed to his decision. The Templars' power and influence, their financial burden on many kingdoms, persistent allegations of heresy and corruption, their involvement in the politics of the Holy Land, and the Pope's personal motives may have all played a role in his decision to dissolve the order. Whatever the reasons, the fall of the Knights Templar marked the end of an era in medieval Europe, and their legacy continues to be felt to this day.

In Portugal, the dissolution of the Templars was not as swift or as severe as in other countries. King Dinis, who had been a supporter of the order, was reluctant to believe the charges against them. He ordered an investigation, but the inquiry was inconclusive, and the Templars continued to operate in Portugal, albeit under a new name: the Order of Christ.

The Order of Christ was created by King Dinis as a successor to the Templars, and it was given many of the same privileges and powers as the old order. However, the Order of Christ was no longer a military order, but a religious one, and its members were more focused on spiritual matters than on military conquest. The Order of Christ was also given control over many of the Templars' former assets, including their lands, castles, and wealth.

Despite the dissolution of the Templars, their influence continued to be felt in Portugal for many years. The Order of Christ, which was founded in their wake, was a powerful and influential organization in its own right. The order was instrumental in the Portuguese voyages of exploration, which brought the country great wealth and prestige in the 15th and 16th centuries. The Templars' legacy also lives on in the art, architecture, and culture of Portugal, which is marked by the unique style of the Templars' buildings and artworks.

The arrest and dissolution of the Templars in Portugal was a turning point in the country's history. While the order was officially dissolved, its legacy lived on through the Order of Christ and other organizations. The Templars' wealth and power helped to shape Portugal's history and left a lasting impact on the country's culture and identity.

THE TEMPLARS' PERSECUTION AND MARTYRDOM IN PORTUGAL

The Templars' persecution and martyrdom in Portugal is a complex and tragic chapter in the country's history that highlights the struggle between power, religion, and personal interests. The Templars had been an influential and respected order in Portugal for many years, and their sudden and unjust persecution was a shock to many.

In Portugal, the Templars' persecution was not as severe as in other countries. King Dinis, who had been a supporter of the order, was hesitant to believe the charges against them. He even attempted to protect the order by issuing a royal decree in 1308 that prohibited anyone from arresting or prosecuting the Templars without his express permission. However, his efforts were not enough to protect the Templars from the eventual dissolution of their order.

Despite the king's support, many Templars in Portugal were still subjected to harsh treatment. They were arrested, interrogated, and tortured until they made false confessions or implicated their fellow Templars. The most common charge against the Templars was that they engaged in heretical practices, such as worshipping idols or committing acts of sodomy. However, these charges were baseless, and were likely fabricated in order to discredit and undermine the order.

One of the most famous cases of Templar persecution in Portugal was that of Friar António. Friar António was a member of the Order of Christ, which was founded to replace the Templars. He was accused of heresy, blasphemy, and other crimes, and he was subjected to a brutal interrogation by the Inquisition. Despite being innocent of the charges against him, Friar António was convicted and burned at the stake in 1539.

Another famous case of Templar persecution in Portugal was that of Friar Amador Arrais. Friar Amador was a member of the Order of Christ, and he was accused of heresy, apostasy, and other crimes by the Inquisition. He was arrested and subjected to a brutal interrogation, and he eventually died in prison. His trial and execution were widely criticized, and they helped to fuel popular opposition to the Inquisition.

Despite the persecution and martyrdom of many of its members, the Templars' legacy lived on in Portugal. The Order of Christ, which was founded to replace the Templars, continued to operate and exert influence in Portugal for many years. The order was instrumental in the Portuguese voyages of exploration, which brought the country great wealth and prestige in the 15th and 16th centuries.

Today, the Templars' persecution and martyrdom are remembered and commemorated in Portugal. The famous Convent of Christ in Tomar, which was once a Templar stronghold, is now a UNESCO World Heritage site that attracts many visitors each year. The Templars' legacy lives on in the country's culture and identity, and they are remembered as courageous defenders of faith and warriors of history.

THE TEMPLARS' SECRET TREASURE AND ITS ALLEGED CONNECTION TO PORTUGAL

The idea of a secret treasure hidden by the Knights Templar has captivated people's imagination for centuries. While there is no concrete evidence that the Templars had such a treasure, many stories and legends have been passed down through the ages.

One of the most intriguing tales is that the Templars, after the dissolution of their order, took their wealth and possessions with them to Portugal. This is based on the fact that many Templars found refuge in Portugal, where they were welcomed by King Dinis, who saw the value in their knowledge and expertise.

The Templars continued to manage their wealth and possessions through a new organization, the Order of Christ, which was established in Portugal. The Order of Christ took over many of the Templars' properties and assets, and its members continued to operate in secret, just as the Templars had done before.

One theory is that the Templars' treasure was not just a collection of gold and silver, but also included priceless artifacts such as religious relics, manuscripts, and works of art. It is believed that the treasure also contained knowledge and secrets that the Templars had acquired during their many years of travel and exploration.

The legend of the Templars' treasure in Portugal centers around the town of Tomar, where the Order of Christ established its headquarters. It is said that the treasure is hidden somewhere in the underground tunnels and chambers beneath the Convent of Christ, a vast complex of buildings that was constructed on the site of the former Templar castle.

Many attempts have been made over the years to find the Templars' treasure in Portugal, but none have been successful so far. Some people believe that the treasure is protected by a curse or other supernatural forces, while others think that it has already been discovered and quietly sold off by those who found it.

Despite the lack of concrete evidence, the legend of the Templars' treasure in Portugal continues to fascinate people to this day. It is a testament to the enduring allure of the Knights Templar and their legacy, which still holds sway over our imaginations even after all these years.

THE LEGACY OF THE TEMPLARS IN PORTUGUESE LITERATURE AND FOLKLORE

The legacy of the Templars in Portuguese literature and folklore is a rich and fascinating one. Although the order was officially dissolved in the 14th century, their influence continued to be felt in Portugal for centuries afterwards.

One of the most famous examples of this legacy is the myth of the Templar treasure. According to legend, the Templars accumulated vast wealth and hid it somewhere in Portugal, possibly in Tomar or in the region of the Algarve. This myth has captured the imagination of the Portuguese people for centuries and has inspired countless stories, poems, and novels.

In the 19th century, the Romantic movement in Portugal helped to revive interest in the Templars and their legacy. Writers such as Alexandre Herculano and Camilo Castelo Branco were among the first to explore the Templars' place in Portuguese history and to incorporate them into their works of fiction.

One of the most famous works of literature to feature the Templars is Herculano's historical novel "The Lusitanian Martyrs" (1845). The novel tells the story of a young Portuguese knight who joins the Templars and is eventually martyred for his faith. The novel's depiction of the Templars as heroic defenders of the faith helped to cement their place in the Portuguese imagination.

Another important work of literature to feature the Templars is Camilo Castelo Branco's novel "The Templars in Portugal" (1878). The novel tells the story of a group of Templars who refuse to disband after the order is officially dissolved and instead go into hiding, living secret lives as protectors of the people. The novel's depiction of the Templars as courageous and noble defenders of the people's rights helped to reinforce their mythic status in Portuguese folklore.

The Templars have also had a lasting impact on Portuguese architecture and art. The most famous example of this is the Convent of Christ in Tomar, which was built on the site of the Templars' original fortress. The convent is a masterpiece of Portuguese architecture and is considered to be one of the country's most important national monuments.

In addition to the Convent of Christ, there are many other examples of Templar influence in Portuguese art and architecture. For example, many Portuguese churches and cathedrals feature Templar motifs and symbols, such as the Maltese cross and the red and white flag.

Overall, the Templars have left a deep and enduring imprint on Portuguese culture. Their legacy can be seen in literature, art, architecture, and folklore, and their memory continues to be celebrated and commemorated to this day.

THE TEMPLARS' INFLUENCE ON PORTUGUESE CULTURE AND SOCIETY

The influence of the Templars on Portuguese culture and society is profound and far-reaching. Although the Order of the Knights Templar was dissolved in Portugal in the 14th century, their legacy lives on in numerous ways. From the iconic architecture of the Convent of Christ to the country's folk traditions, the Templars' presence is felt throughout Portugal.

One of the most significant ways in which the Templars influenced Portuguese culture was through their role in the Reconquista. The Order played a crucial part in the Christian reconquest of the Iberian Peninsula, which had been under Muslim control for centuries. Their valor and skill on the battlefield earned them the respect and admiration of the Portuguese people, and they became celebrated heroes of the nation's history.

The Templars' influence can also be seen in Portugal's architecture. The Convent of Christ in Tomar, which was originally built by the Order, is one of the country's most iconic and impressive structures. The building's mix of Romanesque, Gothic, and Manueline styles reflects the Templars' long history in Portugal and their contribution to the development of Portuguese architecture.

The Templars also left their mark on Portuguese folklore and mythology. Legends abound of Templars hiding treasure throughout the country, and these stories have captured the imagination of generations of Portuguese people. The idea of hidden Templar treasure has become a part of the national identity and is a popular theme in literature and film.

The Templars' influence on Portuguese culture is not limited to the past, either. Today, the Order continues to be celebrated in festivals and events throughout the country. In the town of Tomar, for example, the Festa dos Tabuleiros (Festival of the Trays) is held every four years in honor of the Templars. The festival features elaborate processions and parades that hark back to the Order's medieval heyday.

Finally, the Templars have had a lasting impact on Portuguese society. The Order's legacy of chivalry, bravery, and loyalty continues to be admired and emulated by the Portuguese people. The Templars' commitment to helping others and defending the weak has become a part of the national character, and their influence can be seen in the Portuguese people's commitment to social justice and humanitarian causes.

The Templars' influence on Portuguese culture and society is profound and wide-ranging. Their legacy can be seen in Portugal's architecture, literature, folklore, and festivals. The Order's values of chivalry, bravery, and loyalty continue to inspire the Portuguese people today.

THE TEMPLARS' ROLE IN PORTUGUESE NAVIGATION AND MARITIME EXPANSION

The Templars played a crucial role in Portugal's maritime expansion during the Age of Discovery. As an order with vast resources and knowledge, they were able to contribute greatly to Portugal's growing power and influence as a seafaring nation.

One of the most significant ways in which the Templars contributed to Portugal's maritime expansion was through their knowledge of shipbuilding and navigation. They were renowned shipbuilders and had a deep understanding of the principles of sailing. This expertise allowed them to create better and more efficient vessels, which were crucial to Portugal's maritime success. The Templars also had extensive knowledge of the stars and how to navigate using them. This allowed Portuguese sailors to explore new territories and chart previously unknown waters.

In addition to their expertise in shipbuilding and navigation, the Templars were also instrumental in financing Portugal's maritime endeavors. They had vast financial resources, and their extensive banking system allowed them to provide loans to the Portuguese crown to fund their expeditions. Without the Templars' financial backing, Portugal may not have been able to achieve the level of maritime success that it did.

The Templars were also deeply involved in Portugal's exploration and colonization of new territories. They accompanied many of the Portuguese expeditions as advisers, providing knowledge and expertise on navigation, trade, and other matters. The Templars were often seen as a symbol of Portuguese power and influence in the territories that they explored and colonized.

Their involvement in exploration and colonization was not without controversy, however. Some Templars were accused of exploiting the native populations in the territories that they explored and colonized. Additionally, their involvement in the slave trade and other unethical practices led to criticisms of their actions.

Despite these criticisms, the Templars' contribution to Portuguese navigation and maritime expansion was significant. They played a key role in Portugal's rise to become a world power, and their influence can still be felt today in the country's seafaring culture and maritime industries.

The Templars were instrumental in Portugal's maritime expansion during the Age of Discovery. Their expertise in shipbuilding and navigation, financial power, and involvement in exploration and colonization played a crucial role in Portugal's rise to become a world power. While their actions were not always without controversy, their legacy in Portuguese culture and society remains strong to this day.

THE TEMPLARS' CONNECTION TO THE PORTUGUESE DISCOVERIES AND THE NEW WORLD

The Portuguese discoveries of the 15th and 16th centuries are known for their great geographical and scientific advancements, which helped to expand the boundaries of human knowledge and led to the establishment of vast overseas empires. But what many people may not know is that the Knights Templar played a significant role in these endeavors, both through their earlier explorations of the Mediterranean and through their involvement in the early stages of Portuguese maritime expansion.

One of the most prominent Templars associated with Portuguese exploration is Prince Henry the Navigator, a grandson of King John I and a major patron of Portuguese maritime endeavors in the 15th century. Henry is often credited with launching Portugal's Age of Discovery, but it is less widely known that he was also a member of the Knights Templar, having been initiated into the order in 1418.

Under Prince Henry's patronage, Portuguese explorers began to push south along the West African coast, in search of new trade routes and territories. By the mid-15th century, they had reached the mouth of the Congo River and were trading with the kingdoms of the interior. Then, in 1488, the explorer Bartolomeu Dias rounded the southern tip of Africa and proved that a sea route to the Indian Ocean was indeed possible.

But the Templars' influence on Portuguese exploration didn't end there. When King Manuel I succeeded to the throne in 1495, he inherited a nation on the cusp of major expansion. He also inherited a significant number of Templar knights who had survived the dissolution of the order and were living in Portugal under various names and affiliations.

Many of these former Templars found new purpose and employment in the Portuguese royal court and navy. They brought with them their skills in navigation, cartography, and military strategy, and helped to establish Portugal as a major naval power. One of the most prominent of these Templar expatriates was Diogo Cão, who is credited with discovering the Congo River and charting a large portion of the West African coast.

But the influence of the Templars on Portuguese exploration didn't stop at the African coast. Many historians have pointed to evidence that the Templars may have had knowledge of the New World long before Columbus's famous voyage in 1492. Some have suggested that Templar ships may have sailed to North America as early as the 12th century, and that they may have established a presence in what is now Nova Scotia.

These theories remain controversial, and the evidence is not conclusive. But the idea that the Templars may have had a hand in the discovery of the New World is tantalizing, and has captured the imagination of many people. Whether or not there is any truth to these claims, it is clear that the legacy of the Templars lives on in the great explorations and discoveries of the Age of Discovery, and in the enduring cultural and spiritual connections between

Portugal and the New World.

Knight Templars and the Discovery of Brazil

Pedro Alvares Cabral is a well-known name in Portuguese history, as he is credited with discovering Brazil in 1500 while he was leading a fleet to India. However, little is known about his connection to the Knight Templars.

It is believed that Cabral was a member of the Order of Christ, which was a successor to the Templars in Portugal. The Order of Christ was established in 1319 by King Denis I of Portugal, who granted the Templars' assets and properties to a new order of knights. The order was officially recognized by the pope in 1323 and played a significant role in Portugal's maritime expansion in the 15th and 16th centuries.

Cabral's family had a long history of service to the Portuguese monarchy and the military orders. His father, Fernão Cabral, was the governor of Beira and a Knight of the Order of Aviz, one of the military orders that existed in Portugal at the time. It is likely that Cabral's family connections played a significant role in his appointment as the commander of the second Portuguese India Armada.

The Order of Christ, to which Cabral was affiliated, played a vital role in the Portuguese discoveries and maritime expansion. The order was responsible for funding many of the voyages of exploration and for supporting the development of navigation and cartography. The order also had a significant influence on Portuguese culture and society, with many of its members contributing to the country's literature, art, and architecture.

There is no concrete evidence to suggest that Cabral was directly influenced by the Templars or that he was a member of the order. However, it is possible that he was aware of the order's history and its connection to the Templars, as the Order of Christ was often associated with the Templars.

While there is no concrete evidence to suggest that Pedro Alvares Cabral was directly connected to the Knight Templars, his family's affiliation with the military orders and his membership in the Order of Christ suggests that he was aware of their history and legacy. The influence of the Templars on the Order of Christ, and the role of the order in Portugal's maritime expansion, undoubtedly played a significant role in the country's history and in the history of European exploration.

THE TEMPLARS' INFLUENCE ON THE PORTUGUESE LANGUAGE AND LINGUISTICS

The legacy of the Knight Templars in Portugal goes far beyond their military and political influence. The Order also left its mark on the Portuguese language and linguistics, which is still present to this day.

The Templars, like many other religious orders, were educated men who were well-versed in Latin and other European languages. They used Latin as the language of the Church and for communication with other orders and the Papacy. However, the Templars also adopted local languages in the regions where they settled, including Portuguese.

One of the most significant contributions of the Templars to the Portuguese language was the introduction of new vocabulary related to the military, agriculture, and religion. The Templars were experts in warfare and played a crucial role in the Reconquista, and therefore, they brought many words and expressions related to the art of war, such as "alcácer," "alcáçova," "alcáide," and "arrábido," which are still used in the Portuguese language. The Templars also played an essential role in agriculture and introduced new techniques and terminology to the Portuguese people. For example, the word "latifúndio" (large estate) has its roots in the Latin term "latus fundus," which was used by the Templars to refer to their vast agricultural lands.

The Templars also played a crucial role in the spread of Christianity in Portugal and brought with them many new religious terms and concepts, which enriched the

Portuguese language. Some of the religious terminology introduced by the Templars includes "advento" (advent), "comunhão" (communion), "catecismo" (catechism), "epístola" (epistle), and "salmos" (psalms).

Furthermore, the Templars had a significant influence on Portuguese place-names, which can still be seen today. The Templars founded several villages and towns in Portugal, which they named according to their religious beliefs, and many of these names have been preserved. For example, the village of Sertã, which was founded by the Templars in the 12th century, is named after the Latin word "sertum," which means a wreath or garland of flowers, and is a reference to the crown of thorns worn by Jesus Christ.

In addition to introducing new vocabulary and place-names, the Templars also influenced the development of the Portuguese language in other ways. The Templars were known for their meticulous record-keeping, and they used written documents extensively. They introduced the use of parchment and other writing materials to Portugal, and they also developed a form of shorthand to aid in the speedy transcription of documents.

Moreover, the Templars' use of Latin and other European languages in their communication with other orders and the Papacy also helped to enrich the Portuguese language. Through contact with other languages, Portuguese absorbed new words and expressions, which helped to expand its vocabulary and improve its grammar.

The Templars' influence on the Portuguese language and linguistics was significant and enduring. They introduced new vocabulary related to the military, agriculture, and religion, which enriched the Portuguese language. They also had a significant impact on Portuguese place-names and played a role in the development of Portuguese writing and shorthand. The Templars' contribution to the Portuguese language is a testament to their legacy, which continues to influence Portuguese culture and society to this day.

THE TEMPLARS' MILITARY TACTICS AND EQUIPMENT

The Templars were renowned for their military prowess and innovative tactics, which allowed them to successfully defend and expand Christendom's borders in the Holy Land and beyond. Their strategies were a result of their rigorous training, discipline, and access to the latest weaponry and equipment.

One of the most significant advantages that the Templars had was their use of cavalry. Their knights were trained to fight on horseback, and they were equipped with heavy armor and weapons, including the longsword and lance. The Templars' use of cavalry was particularly effective against the Muslim armies of the time, who relied heavily on lightly armed and mobile horsemen. The heavy charge of the Templar knights was often enough to break the enemy lines and create a gap in their defenses.

In addition to their use of cavalry, the Templars were also known for their unique formation and tactics. They often fought in a tightly packed formation called a "conroi," which allowed them to maximize the strength of their cavalry charges. The conroi was essentially a column of knights, with the most heavily armored and skilled knights in the front ranks. The knights in the rear would use their lances to defend against any attacks from the flanks, while the knights in the front would use their lances to break the enemy lines.

The Templars were also innovative in their use of

fortifications. They built a network of castles and fortresses across the Holy Land, which allowed them to control key strategic locations and defend against enemy attacks. These fortresses were often built on high ground, with thick walls and towers that provided a clear view of the surrounding terrain. The Templars also used moats, drawbridges, and other defensive features to make their fortresses more difficult to attack.

Another aspect of the Templars' military prowess was their use of advanced weaponry. They were among the first European armies to use crossbows, which gave them a significant advantage over the Muslim armies, who relied on traditional bows. The Templars also used siege engines, such as trebuchets and catapults, to break through enemy fortifications.

The Templars' military equipment was also highly advanced for the time. Their armor was designed to provide maximum protection while still allowing for mobility. They wore a chainmail hauberk, which covered their torso and arms, and a helmet that protected their head and neck. They also wore a surcoat or tabard, which displayed the distinctive red cross of the order. The Templars' armor was heavy, but it was also highly effective at protecting them from enemy attacks.

In addition to their armor, the Templars carried a variety of weapons, including the aforementioned longsword and lance. They also carried a small shield, which they could use for protection during close combat. Some knights also carried a mace, which was a heavy club with spikes on the end. The mace was particularly effective against heavily armored opponents.

The Templars' military tactics and equipment were a significant factor in their success on the battlefield. They were able to adapt to changing conditions and new technologies, which allowed them to maintain their advantage over their enemies. Today, their tactics and equipment continue to be studied by military historians and enthusiasts, and their legacy lives on in popular culture and in the modern-day Knights Templar organizations.

THE TEMPLARS' LEGACY AND IMPACT ON MILITARY ORDERS IN EUROPE

The Templars, with their impressive military power and financial influence, left a lasting legacy on European history. They established the model of the military order, which was soon followed by other orders such as the Hospitallers, the Teutonic Knights, and the Order of Santiago. These orders imitated the Templars' organization, rules, and military tactics.

The legacy of the Templars was not limited to the military sphere, but also extended to the cultural and social aspects of European life. The Templars' involvement in the Crusades introduced Europe to the Islamic world, and the cultural exchange that followed had a profound impact on the development of European art, literature, and philosophy.

Furthermore, the Templars' banking system and financial power also had a lasting impact on European commerce and economics. They established a network of branches throughout Europe, which facilitated trade and investment. The Templars also introduced the concept of credit, and their financial system was a precursor to modern banking.

The dissolution of the Templars in the early 14th century did not end their legacy. The surviving members of the order joined other military orders, and their knowledge and experience continued to be passed down through the generations. The model of the military order that they established also influenced the development of secular armies and the modern concept of the nation-state.

The Templars' legacy can still be seen in the cultural and social aspects of European life, including literature, art, and architecture. Many European cities still have buildings and monuments that were built by the Templars, and their influence can also be seen in the traditions and folklore of many European countries.

The Templars were not only a powerful military force, but they also had a significant impact on European culture, commerce, and society. Their legacy continues to influence and inspire people today, and their contributions to European history will never be forgotten.

THE LEGACY OF THE TEMPLARS IN MODERN-DAY PORTUGAL AND THE WORLD

The legacy of the Templars can still be felt today, not only in Portugal but also in other parts of the world. Their influence on the Portuguese culture, language, and society has been significant and long-lasting, and their impact on military orders in Europe cannot be underestimated.

One of the most visible legacies of the Templars in Portugal is the wealth of architectural and artistic treasures they left behind. The castle of Tomar, with its remarkable round church and convent, is a UNESCO World Heritage site and one of the most important examples of Templar architecture in Europe. The Convent of Christ in Tomar, which was founded by the Order of Christ in the 14th century, is another significant example of the Templars' influence on Portuguese art and architecture. Many other churches and chapels throughout Portugal bear witness to the Templars' artistic and religious legacy.

The Templars also left an indelible mark on the Portuguese language, particularly in the areas of naval and military terminology. Words such as "almirante" (admiral), "armada" (fleet), and "esquadra" (squadron) all have their roots in the Portuguese language and reflect the country's maritime heritage. These words are still used today not only in Portugal but also in many other languages around the world.

The Templars' influence on Portuguese society can also be seen in the country's tradition of religious processions and festivals. The Feast of the Holy Spirit, which is celebrated in many parts of Portugal, is a vivid example of the Templars' legacy. This festival, which dates back to the 14th century, is marked by processions and the distribution of bread and wine to the poor. The tradition of the Holy Ghost processions has also spread to other parts of the world, including the United States and Canada, where Portuguese immigrants have carried on this cultural practice.

The Templars' influence on military orders in Europe is also significant. The Order of Christ, which was founded in Portugal after the dissolution of the Templars, became one of the most important military orders in Europe. Its members included some of the greatest explorers and navigators of the age of discovery, such as Vasco da Gama and Pedro Álvares Cabral. The Order of Christ played a crucial role in Portugal's maritime expansion and the exploration of the New World.

The Templars' legacy has also had a lasting impact on popular culture and media. Books, movies, and TV shows about the Templars continue to captivate audiences around the world. Their story of bravery, devotion, and loyalty continues to inspire people to this day.

Templars' influence on Portuguese culture, language, society, and military orders cannot be overstated. Their legacy can still be felt today in Portugal and beyond, and their impact on history has been immense. The Templars were not only warriors and defenders of the faith, but they were also builders, artists, and explorers. Their legacy is a testament to their enduring influence on the world.

....

END.

www.ingramcontent.com/pod-product-compliance
Ingram Content Group UK Ltd.
Pitfield, Milton Keynes, MK11 3LW, UK
UKHW022010190726
13853UKWH00004B/1850